© The Opiate Books 2024
Cover art: "Nymphs Dancing to Pan's Flute" by Joseph Tomanek
ISBN: 978-2-9593278-1-0

"The way to maintain one's connection to the wild is to ask yourself what it is that you want. This is the sorting of the seed from the dirt."
-**Clarissa Pinkola Estés,** *Women Who Run With the Wolves*

"Look at the wealth of data concealed in the grid, in the bright packaging, the jingles, the slice-of-life commercials, the products hurtling out of the darkness, the coded messages and endless repetitions, like chants, like mantras. 'Coke is it, Coke is it, Coke is it.'"
-**Don DeLillo,** *White Noise*

"I've been runnin' on stardust/Alone for so long/I wouldn't know what hot fire was."
-**Lana Del Rey, "Wildflower Wildfire"**

Table of Contents

Foreword 1

[all neon lights] 3

[pankow] 4

[polaroid] 7

[1999] 8

[cat person] 9

[sparrow] 10

[saigon] 11

[stargirl] 12

[beautiful losers] 13

[cinema italiano, where are you now?] 14

[honest poem] 15

[badlands] 16

[pop] 17

[glitch] 18

[incandescent adolescent] 19

[cut] 20

[99¢ dreams] 21

[family portrait] 22

[flux] 23

[animals] 24

[boxes] 25

[mama e su soli] 26

[august 3rd, 6 a.m., italy] 27

[honey jar] 29

[longing] 30

[girls-girls-girls] 31
[lust] 32
[the lotus brothel] 33
[the genius' wife] 34
[heavenly] 35
[ghost] 36
[spiders] 37
[control] 38
[seek and destroy] 40
[low serotonin] 41
[I want to be a sunset] 42
[howl reloaded] 43
[paris, paris] 44
[three a.m.] 45
[burn] 46
[nice man] 47
[stendhal syndrome] 48
[parisian taxi driver] 49
[west london, 7 a.m.] 50
[underground] 51
[porntry] 52
[the waitress with the roman nose] 53
[heroin] 54
[molotov] 55
[all I need] 56
[little tokyo] 57
[my pulse] 58

[sad girl pop] 59
[overdrive] 60
[antisocial] 61
[#idiosyncrasy] 62
[pigs] 63
[iconoclast] 64
[hello] 65
[somedays] 66
[purge] 67
[birds] 68
[black coffee] 69
[washing machines] 70
[closed for inventory] 71
[this is not a poem] 72
[butterflies underground] 73
[life choices on sunday morning] 74
[to-do list] 75
[last prayer] 76
[light blue] 77
[astrophilia] 78

Foreword

It's not an easy thing, to be raw. Really and truly *raw*—like a goddamn piece of sushi. To display the kind of unbridled fire that, more and more, everyone (not just those in positions of power) wants to see stamped out. Or at least "controlled." But there are some flames that can't be tamed. And, on that note, while most poets of the present shy away from embodying true grit—from making the reader "uncomfortable" by presenting them with "too many" emotions—Chiara Maxia displays the kind of passion and spiritedness so sorely lacking in modern poetry.

In addition to simultaneously enchanting and astounding the reader with her singular voice, there are also many moments throughout Maxia's *The Fire Within* that might remind one of certain other major names in postmodern literature (and even some names that are "pre," such as Dorothy Parker). Allen Ginsberg, for one. Yet it's the postmodern prowess of Don DeLillo (see: the collection's opening poem, "all neon lights," and, later, "99¢ dreams") that Maxia's work often epitomizes. Not to mention the fatalistic romanticism of Lana Del Rey.

Said chanteuse flickers in during a few of Maxia's more "we're in decay"-themed poems, including "flux," wherein she writes, "Off-license beauty queens live on CCTV/neon makeup liquefied in alcohol and tears/monitors can't believe the state we are in." Or on "little tokyo," when "heaven is a night on earth with you" subs in for the more derivative line from "Video Games" that goes, "Heaven is a place on Earth with you." Even Maxia's razor-sharp, beacon-of-self-awareness "sad girl pop" is what best describes Del Rey's genre, with Maxia one-upping the "Body Electric" lyric, "Mary prays the rosary for my broken mind" by describing, "He's a dagger in my head/that fills the crack of my broken mind."

But if this is what a broken mind looks like, then one can only pray for many more like Maxia's on this planet that instead puts a premium on "healthy" minds. Because no so-called healthy brain could appreciate the work of Vincent Gallo, could it? As Maxia alludes to in "all i need" when she casually announces, "You're all I need/my cinematic bad man/I'll be your brown bunny."

The sensual nature of Maxia's poetry is equalled only by the blasé manner in which she cuts the objects of her potential affection like a knife. The best of both worlds is on full display in the unforgettable "pankow." In it, Maxia muses on a chance encounter that perfectly illuminates how, for many of us, the idea of what someone *could* be is far more worth clinging to than actually seeing where a dalliance might lead if allowed to continue for a few more days…or even just a few more hours.

Striking such resonant chords with the disconnect between our fantasies versus our crippling, unwanted realities, Maxia's is a voice that ultimately stands all on its own as it commingles the best of all possible influences.

Genna Rivieccio
Editor, The Opiate Books
Summer 2024

[all neon lights]

there's nothing human in working ten hours a day, five days a week
to make money for someone else.

COCA-COLA MEANS I LOVE YOU

or to drive forty-five minutes to go and forty-five to return.

JUST DO IT

especially when it rains.

BECAUSE YOU'RE WORTH IT

like that scene from *The Deer Hunter*, but I paid for the bullet.

THINK DIFFERENT

how long have I been stuck here?

IT'S FINGER-LICKING GOOD

this can't be real.

I CAN'T BELIEVE IT'S NOT BUTTER

this isn't reality.

SPEED LIMIT 45MPH
YOUR SPEED 86MPH
SLOW DOWN
SLOW DOWN
SLOW DOWN
SL—

[pankow]

What am I doing in this apartment with you.

The sky above Berlin is gray, the colors are sharp and dark. You fell asleep and your laptop keeps on looping a video of a 1930s cartoon whose black and white characters dance spasmodically to barely hearable techno music. Above you, there are pencil-drawn sketches mounted on the wall in the form of a storyboard. On your right, a chair with your clothes on it. On your left, the floor is an obstacle course of ashtrays, lighters, books, bottles of Sterni and Club-Mate until the desk on which you give birth to your creations.

I met you on the train. You're mute. The fact that you wanted to communicate with me got me intrigued. Firstly, an alphabet of glances in the distance, then closer, then writing in German on a notebook. And to find out you had no other words to write in another language looked like a passionating challenge with mythological nuances. While the train ran silent and fast across continental Europe, we kept on talking: eyes, hands, glances, the few thin words I know in your language, drawings, tappings. Then I followed you in Berlin.

The mating ritual was short, but intense. When the word fails, there's a whole universe screaming in its place. Language is a structure as frail as a sparrow's ribcage, unfit by nature to carry the heaviness of emotions. Even trying in every way and with the best of intentions, feelings cannot be converted into words, it's never the same thing, and that's an objective fact, like: "Water boils at one-hundred degrees Celsius." One of those things you just have to accept.

We ended up on your mattress, looking at each other, communicating with our para-verbal system. I had an orgasm, then another, even if less strong. You too. We cuddled.

At the beginning I was afraid, of course. I had the same fear of every girl grown up in the presence of mother, father, television, school, society. Warning. Beware. Beware of males, beware of strangers, beware of others, beware of everything. It's dangerous, you end up badly, dark alley, ambulance, hospital, morgue, obituary. You could have been anyone. You could have had a murky past casually picked among the thousands of stolen childhoods that subsequently evolve in misfits and malfunctioning adults. You could have been a thief, a killer, a rapist or, at best, a subnormal. Instead, I find out you're none of this.

You smoke weed and tobacco. You read Kundera. You go for groceries in the supermarket two blocks away, preferring vegan and cruelty-free products. You listen to Kraftwerk. You know who Klaus Nomi is, and you know why he's important. You find Bauhaus sublime, as well as the homonymous post-punk band. You love yoga, you hate fast-food restaurants. You're an artist. We're similar. You're not dangerous. You're not a maniac. You're not a thief. You're nothing. And after forty-eight hours, in spite of the linguistic impediment, we've already run out of things to say to each other. The bitter truth is that, if I knew German and your phonetic apparatus worked, we would have run out of them in less than two hours.

What am I doing in this apartment with you.

I smoke a cigarette looking out of the window. I watch the afternoon sky, the buildings, the street, bicycles, dogs, the Rewe, Turkish kebab shops, the lives of others. I turn around and look at you, in your quiet post-wine and post-sex sleep. I inhale the last drag and stub it out.
I silently collect my belongings. I wear my backpack, my shoulder bag. I walk towards the apartment door and close it behind me. It is the right thing. Better if this short story we created together painlessly slides from sleep to death without having to submit ourselves to the humiliating ritual of goodbyes and explanations.

Stairs, main entrance, U-Bahn. Bye.

[polaroid]

flash.

the colors slowly take shape on the lucid paper:
bushy eyebrows
big lips
dark circles
from lack of sleep.

hazel eyes
looking right in the lens
desperately looking for idols.

scruffy hair
the fire within
five foot three of water
and unsolved things.

as the picture gets clear
a crooked smile appears.

[1999]

I remember the end of the century in photograms
occasionally appearing on a flickering TV screen
I remember the millennium bug
remember to turn off your computer before midnight
I remember President Clinton
Celebrity Deathmatch, Beavis and Butt-Head
a stillborn Tamagotchi, a can of cherry cola
The Columbine High School massacre
I remember the general blame on violent video games
South Park, Marilyn Manson
I remember Windows 95, Blockbuster
sellers on cable TV screaming at the top of their lungs
their teeth as white and sharp as fangs
I remember the sound of dial-up internet
Crash Bandicoot and *Tomb Raider*
a tower of floppy disks and amateur videotapes
the harmless taste of strawberry milkshake
the sugar rash chewing on a Big Babol
as I was learning
to put the alphabet together
letters to read
letters to write.

[cat person]

it's a truth universally acknowledged that dogs are better
than cats—
some say better than humans too, but that's a whole
different story, don't want to go there—
dog eyes don't have a soulless cut in the middle like cats'
have
they'll risk their own life for their owner's
understand more words than any other species (some
voters included).

despite all of this I'm not a dog person
or I might be—let's say I identify as nonbinary.

dogs stay no matter how low you stoop
they adore you at your worst as much as at your best
they jump in ecstasy every time you get back home, and
that's enough already—
I can't deal with that much love.

[sparrow]

you say I'm not girlfriend material
you're probably right
your wife used to be a girlfriend too
and look at her now:

wishing she had half of your ego,
waiting,
forcing herself to believe you are where you told her you
were going
while you play with my hair and tell me
how stupid and obnoxious she is.

I certainly don't want to end up
gray, wilted and fat,
pouring myself a pint of soda
and thinking about the times when
I was pretty and had something interesting to say.

you say I'm not girlfriend material,
I deserve much better than that.
you're probably right, I think,
while you call me your little sparrow and crack my wings
with your heavy hands.

I pity her
as I pity myself
and make that smirk you love so much.

[saigon]

his heart's a place where reality has long been forgotten
it pumps fire and hard metals, they get to his head
giving him napalm eyes, a Russian roulette smile

his knotty hands are on my shoulders, he could
snap my neck any moment
I crumble and slip through his fingers

landing in his rough hands
like the poisoned sand of the Mekong River
I have long lost the game
but he loves me
like my demons do.

[stargirl]

I appear mirrored in the lens he uses
to watch me without looking.
behind the camera
his eyes open and close,
his skin crinkles
his rough fingers caress gently
my naked image on the screen.

touching me from a distance
with his chain-smoker breath
and his cavernous voice
muttering to himself
"stargirl, stargirl."

I move and breathe on his blue sofa
alive but not there
a muse is never human
she is a concept
burning violently in his head.

[beautiful losers]

my quarter-life crisis
and your midlife crisis
perfectly fit each other.

[cinema italiano, where are you now?]

I don't have a TV in my apartment
but it's not like I'm proud of that
I'm just stating a fact like
I prefer coffee over tea or
I'm not a big football fan.

still, when I visit my family in Italy
I grab their remote and soak in the ether
up to my neck in the radio waves.

they thank us for paying for the service
between what the Pope said today and the latest sex
scandal
couples reuniting after a lifetime of pain, gasping in hugs
and spasmodic tears —
and you should say it with Pandora —

families around the breakfast table talking to each other
unsynchronised voiceovers
riots, protests, mafia, revenge porn
monsters of catholic imagination.

people getting married in tasteless opulence
with cameras filming them, amused and judgmental 'cause
everyone has got an opinion and
everyone is screaming so loud
and I'm in love with this Fellinian freak show
'cause I'm no better than them
we're all lost in a cup of espresso.

[honest poem]

write about what you know, he says
right, sir.

I know what's the capital city of Moldova
I know two plus two equals four, but if I say five it shows
I've read Orwell.

I know my navel has a funny shape
I know the NHS underfunding is the one to blame.

I know my eyes turn green when I cry
though it happens quite rarely (for which I take pride).

I know I'm still hurt but can't remember what for
I know the best insult I got was "Bolshevik whore."

I know where I come from, I know someday this will end
I don't know what's happening, but that makes perfect
sense.

[badlands]

nobody can love the Mediterranean badlands
as much as under a leaden sky full of resentment.

with the black sea roaring in the distance
breaking its waves on opalescent rocks
with plants finding their way back
through nude bricks and broken asphalt
under a V of birds flying low

with loners rambling on the dirt roads
sand and stones, homes of scorpios and hermit crabs
fishermen waiting alone on the shore
with their jeans full of splinters
and their skin full of salt

nobody can love the Mediterranean badlands
as much as under a leaden sky full of resentment.

[pop]

"princesses don't smoke"
said the elder passerby while I was inhaling
quite satisfied my post-Diet Coke cigarette

you never know what to reply to statements like this
(right? wrong?
I'm no princess?)
but luckily I didn't have to—
he just spoke his mind and carried on with his life

I drank the last drop of soda
looked at the boats waving in the harbor
stubbed out my cigarette
grabbed my bag and walked away.

[glitch]

amateur videotapes
show 90s babies
eating ice cream at the zoo
animals in cages
the adults are happy.

[incandescent adolescent]

two fingers down my throat for I take up too much space
the other two to make the thought of him go away
five nails deep in my skin to plead my body guilty
a punch right in my guts 'cause I am
bad
and
filthy.

[cut]

disfigure the already imperfect—
dirty, hideous, filthy
rotten, gunky, unworthy—
butcher of teenage meat
master of common-use blades
she cuts herself open
skin layers disclosing like eyelids
crying slowly
in the towels, toilet paper
heavy drops down the freshly-scrubbed tiles
steaming hot blood
on the cold marble floor.

[99¢ dreams]

twilight on the parking lot
objects in mirror are closer than they appear
objects of desire are closer than they appear
shopping windows reflect demons
laughing back at us
selling fast fashion
expensive visions of hell
Sony screens broadcast
female bodies made in Taiwan
opening their legs in 4K

peppermint-flavored, pocket-size Virgin Marys
Jesus-shaped popsicles to melt in
mouths thirsty for salvation and cheap thrills
out-of-stock American dreams
we inhale neon dust
we exhale dirt
and one by one we drop dead.

[family portrait]

Uncle Bob was a bit of a snob
("dick" would be more fitting but I wanted the first line to rhyme)
he used to say that men with class don't need a glass
while spending his wife's money on gambling and girls.

Auntie Barb was such a cunt, worse than the devil himself.
Auntie Pattie her younger sister, too rich of devotion and too poor of intellect
to recognize her sadistic intrigues.

Uncle Conor was a big moron—but honest, at least.
Auntie Lauren never recovered from the time
Auntie Mae hit her on the head.
Uncle Eamon was born a demon, and his children learned that quickly.
Uncle Hugh was nothing but screwed
but they say, you know,
there's never one point of view.

[flux]

heaven lit by convenience store lights
we dance to FM 100 Islamabad
parading between Cadbury treats and a wall of beer cans
we twist and turn in the flicker like moths
like baby bats drenched in Jägerbombs

pills in our eyes, star crowns on our heads
Saturn rings orbiting around our stitched wrists
off-license beauty queens live on CCTV

neon makeup liquefied in alcohol and tears
monitors can't believe the state we are in
Eurotrash night bugs playing hide-and-seek
among canned soup, beer, expired crisp packs
our skin tonight will die behind us.

[animals]

two seventeen-year-olds
walk around the summer wasteland
in a distorted afternoon
their skin sunburnt
their eyes green of sun.

stray dogs
thirsty for soda and meanings
hiding in bookshops
dark rooms
basements.

little animals
exploring with their hands
still stained with blue ink
and their mouths
still plump
and their tongues
still clean.

[boxes]

no future, some present, the past.
paper, dust, notebooks from primary school and
their childish essays
legs without their dolls
disposable cam photos
3D glasses I'd get at the cinema
the ultimate cool things of the times before
bus and theater tickets
dirty wristbands,
CDs, audiotapes
diaries
birthday cards
broken things
still waiting to be fixed.

[mama e su soli]

there are days she appears in the roaring heat
like a mirage, but awfully real
her naked feet on the burning cobblestones
her hay blond hair shining in the ultraviolent rays
eyes of liquid fire, snake-like teeth
glimmering of appetite

there are days nobody is there for the rescue of children
she grabs them in her claws
holding tight she takes them away
somewhere over the sun.

[august 3rd, 6 a.m., italy]

Eyes. Open. Up. In.the.smooth.morning.light.
The.summer.appears. I.don't.look.in.the.mirror. I
don't.brush.my.hair. I.leave.the.house.
From.the.kitchen.door. Silently. Fast.
I.walk.until.the.beach.

In.the.sandy.distance.there.are.a.few.spare.fishermen.
They're.waiting.for.preys.to.raise.to.the.bait.
I.often.wonder.what.fishermen.think.
I.often.wonder.if.fishermen.feel.lonely. I. Often. Wonder.
The.sun.is.still.low.
Sometimes.there.are.young.folks.asleep.in.a.line.of.
sleeping.bags.
Next.to.a.line.of.empty.beer.bottles.

I.put.my.towel.down. I.reach.the.water.
I.walk.on.the.pebbles.on.the.foreshore.
Until.the.water.reaches.my.waist. I. Plunge. I. Swim.
I.swim.coasting.the.buoy.line. I.swim.until.the.last.buoy.
Where.the.sea.is.bluer.
And.the.seabed.is.four.or.five.meters.away.
I.take.a.deep.breath.and.go.down.
I.take.a.deep.breath.and.
let.
it.
go.

Fishes.move. Ears.get.clogged.
Arms.and.legs.move.to.touch.the.seabed.
The.world.down.here.is. Silent. Quiet. Hazy.
I.try.to.see.what's.further.

I.can't.see.anything.beside.the.whiteness.of.the.sea.bottom.
and.the.blue.of.the.distance. Blue.
Wherever.I.look.everything.is.blue.
When.I'm.born.again.I.want.to.be.born.blue.
I.twirl.and.I.turn.　I.lift.my.chin.
I.can.see.the.light.seeping.in.through.the.thick.water.blanket. Reflecting.itself.on.my. hands.
Still.pale.from.the.long.winter. I.swim.up. Emerge.
Arms.up. As.I.were.surrendering.to. something.
I.open.my.mouth.and.breathe.again.
The.sun.is.now.higher.
The.sun.shines.too.bright.down.here.
I'm.not.used.to.this.anymore. I.let.it.blind.me.

I.lie.on.the.water. Eyes.to.the.Sky.
The.sky.is.painted.in.colors.that.don't.exist.
I.taste.the.salt.on,my.lips. I.take.another.breath.
Plunge.again. Keep.On.Swimming.

Back.quite.dizzy.on.the.solid.ground.
I.dry.myself.quickly.
I.walk.back.home.
My.coffee.this.morning will.
taste.
like.
the.
Sea.

[honey jar]

your big hands are miles away
somewhere the afternoon is not this torrid and silent
forcing us humans to hide behind the blinders like
cockroaches ashamed of themselves

where you are, the summer air is crispy and fresh
and your knotty fingers play with the dew and breeze
or with the drops beading your pint of cold brew

and your bedsheets are never sweaty
and your blood pressure is high enough
and I hope you think of me too

laid down in the amber shadow
I caress my summer dress
slow motion until the seams
to put my fingers the honey jar
you are not with me
I pretend you are.

[longing]

I want strawberry champagne
springtime to come earlier
my pulse to beat much faster
and those things I've read in books.

[girls-girls-girls]

people want poetry
dripping down the eyes
of a young go-go dancer.

[lust]

green-purple-icy-silver neon lights
on razor-sharp cheekbones
candy-pink slavic doll
eyes as deep as two black holes
remains of alcoholic fathers
and mothers high on the dream of freedom
oh what a wonderful world
somewhere over the wall

//pay me in dollars
groom me pretty and show me off//

look what I found—look what I've got
she loves me because of course she does
I love her because she's mine
eastern beauty, silver birch in the snow
she's a ballerina too
my lust in translation
my little girl blue.

[the lotus brothel]

girls for every taste
girls for every pocket
doe-eyed, cat-eyed, small breasts, big mouths
wide hips, redheads, big blondes, tiny and tall

they fluctuate along the corridors,
gracious around the fine china vases
on the burgundy carpets and by the blue velvet curtains
caressing feathers, flowers and silk

some are at the bar, some are playing by the stairs
some are dancing slowly, pearls rattling around their swan necks
some sit on the knees of clients resting on opulent armchairs
old money, whiskey in one hand, a vague idea of love in the other

where is madame lotus? somebody asks
rampant, self-made trash, no clue whatsoever
too young, too arrogant, no sense of decency
aesthetic or class
first time?
yes.
son, nobody has ever had enough money
or enough flair
and for that matter, neither enough bravery
to even dare asking for the maîtresse.

[the genius' wife]

the genius' wife
is a quiet woman
she is well-read
and smartly dressed
she keeps the place clean
and the children cared for

the genius' wife
stays by her husband's side
she brings him coffee cups
empties the ashtrays
and leaves the studio silently

the genius' wife
has a tiny body
sun-starved pale eyes
a bluebird voice a few could ever hear

the genius' wife
must have an ID somewhere
among the jewels, paperwork and fresh flowers
or maybe up in the attic
it doesn't matter, really
she is the genius' wife.

[heavenly]

nothing more alluring,
compelling, poetic
than a smile appearing
on a black-and-blue upper lip
disclosing on gums
beading with blood.

[ghost]

I can feel it seeping in
getting inside
crawling upwards
hole to heart
I can feel it
most when I'm alone.

[spiders]

they're inside
they must have got in from a hole on the wall
or 'cause I forgot to lock the door
they're all over my kitchen
eating all that's in the cupboard
there's a mass of them in my bedroom
grinding everything that was mine once
they're coming in and out of books and journals
sniggering nastily at my despair
they're running up and down my body
biting hard legs, breasts and arms
they could spend their whole bug life on me
they're having so much fun.

[control]

Lightnings of paranoid white slash open your field of vision. Cold sweat on your body light as air and heavy as a pile of abandoned scrap metal. A dog from hell merciless savages your chest. Modesty aside, I trained it myself.

It's me again, the Demon of Panic. I don't phone, I don't knock at your door. I appear. I have a slight appetite and I want to feast on you, possibly with a side of fava beans and a good Chianti. I arrive when I most feel like it, and that's perfectly fine. Actually, the more I take you by surprise, the better.

I adore the dismay on your chubby baby face. I adore the way you whisper *not-now-it's-okay-it's-okay-it's-okay*. It's not okay at all, and you perfectly know it. You gasp and tremble, hot flushes depart from your kidneys and go up to your brain. Your head hurts, your jaw clenched like an improvised dam against the evil senses. But they're little filiform demons, they rise up to the brain and profane it, tiny neo-Nazis in a punitive expedition because, as the stupid ho you are, you let your guard down and left the door wide open for me. It is your fault, and your fault only.

Your skull pulses and hurts. You're terrorized. Your lungs will collapse. Your heart desperately fights against my mastiff's ruthless teeth. There's no way out. You tighten your fists and start to punch your knees, thighs, hips. Way to go, baby, hurt yourself. Help me in your destruction, with your reddish face disfigured by tears, saliva and cheap mascara, a bad copy of a Picasso made in PRC.

You can't make it. You're alone. The walls are white and you're alone. You're in the void. You shiver, the arms in which you sank your fingernails make your bracelets jangle. You approach the medicine cabinet walking like a wounded animal. Aspirine. Ibuprofen. Paracetamol. Plasters. Antiseptic. Where's the anxiolytic? Where's the opium-based medicine for which you obtained a prescription the week before it got withdrawn from the market? Here. Blister. It's the last pill. The fuck knows how you'll manage next time, if the next one prescribed by that drug dealer in a white coat will be as effective as this one. God knows how you'll curse yourself next time for not having lasted longer today, for not having been able to manage without the powerful pharmaceutical help.

You put the capsule in your mouth. You swallow it. Swallow, you whore. You flush it down with a few drops of tap water from the bathroom sink. Shortly your senses calm down under a warm glaze of legal drug. I fade away little by little. My outlines evaporate until I leave the room. Evanescent.

Volatilized. I'm gone.

But sooner or later I'll come back. And eat you alive.

[seek and destroy]

I seek and destroy and I do it for fun.
I seek and destroy and you'd better run.
I seek and destroy, I love it outrageously.
I seek and destroy and I orgasm spontaneously.

I seek and destroy whatever you love.
I'll kill the embryo in your blooming womb.
I seek and destroy and God's on my side.
I seek and destroy and they'd better hide.

I seek and destroy, your life is not sacred.
I seek and destroy, and you know you deserve it.

[low serotonin]

shielded by the blinders in the air-conditioned room
I see the sun showering the outside world
popsicles melting, skin crinkling around eyes and mouths
sweat dripping from alive beings

in my very own bell jar
the temperature doesn't exceed twenty-two degrees
I'm lost in a lukewarm cup of americano
Bergman is dead and God is unwell too
i'm aseptic clean—
that is not me.

[I want to be a sunset]

laid down on the couch, eyes on the golden hour
I keep my hands from hurting me
smoking away
whispering mantras of cheap new-age production.

I want to be a sunset
I want to be big and warm and beautiful and quiet
I'm just waiting for pigs to fly
as the seagulls come and go
somewhere over the window.

[howl reloaded]

I saw the best minds of my generation
allying with strangers on the internet
against someone they had never heard of
for writing something they had never read
about something that was not their concern
in the first place.

[paris, paris]

picture me in Paris
(any *bistrot* will do)
there's a man in the corner staring at the bubbles going up
his pint
there's a young poet, pastis on his table, beside his
notebook and pen
he's cursing the goddess of inspiration.

There's a lady in jewels and floral perfume
the heavy gems around her neck
bow her head on the counter.

The barman is trying to remember what once the prophet
said
words lost in the Algerian sand
words lost in the city dirt
as the fan spins above the bottles and our heads
and an old song comes in through the doors
wide open in the summer quietness.

I can be alone forever in Paris
I can never be lonely.

[three a.m.]

At three in the morning everything's quiet. Strangely
enough, so am I.
Of course like every insomniac I wish I could sleep
but it's no big deal if I don't.

At three in the morning the neighbours aren't fighting
and the baby next door is asleep
the streets are empty under a glaze of calming darkness
no roaring motors, shouting, shattered glasses.

At three in the morning life is on halt.
Even if I wanted to, I wouldn't be able to go out and run
emotionally draining errands
and spend money to survive.

At three a.m. everything's quiet
I enjoy my lack of sleep in bed
exactly where I'm supposed to be.

[burn]

see me watching you
as the flame runs fast
the photograph burns
there are eyes in your smoke
now they're gone.

dream on…

[nice man]

I am not in love
(never said I was)
I have nothing against you, either

you wear a nice smile
you drive a nice car
you've never slapped me—
a generally decent man

I like sitting by your side
heading southeast
to a picturesque place
where we'll have nothing to say to each other

but I could dance slowly in front of you
be whatever you think I am
while you watch in adoration
fill my glass
and forget who you are.

[stendhal syndrome]

I dreamt of running blindfolded through the Louvre
with white horses galloping behind
silent thunderstorms drumming on the glass windows
Hermitage nymphs in childlike surprise

Warhol silk screens rolling on the walls
terrible angels flying sky-high
on cello solos, harp delicacies
royal arcades, velvet rope rhapsodies

and I was so small twirling in the twilight dome
and I was so small in the infinity room
and little by little I'm fading away
my veins are dripping methylene blue.

[parisian taxi driver]

optimism is the worst drug, mademoiselle.

it eats you slowly,
from the inside.

and in no time you are
old,
and rotten, and aching, and tired,
driving young people
to their shared flats
where they drink, and party, and fuck,
and fall asleep,
and d.r.e.a.m.

[west london, 7 a.m.]

he appears like a mirage
in his black coat and black hat
his coffee to-go exhaling its fumes from
the paper cup in his gloved hand

he doesn't see me
amongst the early morning mist and the running blind
commuters
slaloming around trash cans, ATMs
traffic lights
tube on, tube off

he doesn't realize
there are nails in my bones
pinning me to the pavement
a rabbit heart in my ribcage
or that I fear and tremble
as my eyes get liquid and my mouth gets dry

in a moment the escalator swallows old ladies,
students, Pakistanis
kids in uniforms, Italians and Poles
a multitude of law-suited ants
and he's gone
at 7:01 a.m.

[underground]

how many hours of my life have I spent on these trains.
how many has a pure Londoner.
juggling coins, Oyster cards, dirty copies of the *Evening Standard*,
the *Metro* too,
kicking empty cans.

probably since he can remember
he's been seeing himself in the passengers in front of him:
cold, tired, mildly annoyed
accurately avoiding to make arm or eye contact
at eight a.m., in East London, we all have the same face.

apart from that morning in November
when amazement sat before me:
a fairy-like creature
black features
transparent skin
freckles like stars
as red as his hair
a resting smile
outrageously spontaneous
underground galaxy on fire

the spell ended at Bromley-by-Bow
the aftermath stayed
beauty saved me that day
I know it will again.

[porntry]

I followed the crowd and their coats full of rain until down at the bar
to curl up in first line, my arms around my knees, looking at him up onstage
I greedily swallow his mouth reading about romance and pain
I greedily swallow him with every inch of my overpowered body

his sultry voice on us like smoke over London
the velvety wine in my glass touching my lips as though it was his tongue
he's so handsome, it hurts
his words so strong, I bruise spontaneously

he can have all the girls he wants
I can have all his books of poetry
I can have all my visions of porntry.

[the waitress with the roman nose]

I admire her figure:
graceful as she swings around the tables
cleaning up after the clients, collecting empty glasses,
with an absent gaze, the enlightened type,
hands busy with trivialities
mind closer than ever to the divine

I could stare at her forever
But not in a lustful way,
not even with envy, or admiration, for that matter
I look at her
like I'd look at a Van Gogh,
a burning fire,
an Icelandic waterfall,
a sky full of stars.

[heroin]

I want a man with lips like heroin
I dreamed of him last night—
fell out of bed twice
I want to die in a rash of endorphins
at peace, in love
with very little to regret.

[molotov]

He thinks I can save him.

With my lust for life
taste for classic books and records.
With my old soul trapped in a restless body
who doesn't speak much and sleeps even less.
With notebooks in my purse,
peachy balm in my pocket
and film quotes in my head.

His heart is in my hands.

I'll go out in a blast.

I'm a fragile

        kind
          of
            glass

[all I need]

our tongues rolling like movie reels
caught fire in the midnight sun
we inhale our flower-scented sweat
we exhale velvety fumes
silky smooth on our skin.
you're all I need
my cinematic bad man
I'll be your brown bunny.

[little tokyo]

tonight we could have a little stroll downtown
I'd like to walk along the floor-to-ceiling jellyfish aquarium
you can buy me a robot koi from the toy shop
to swim with me in your king-size tub

we can have dinner at Little Tokyo
buy something with its own culinary philosophy
use golden chopsticks Freddy Krueger-style
eat in silence, our awestruck eyes on the screen
broadcasting the crowning of Broadcaster of the Year

I admire your style and manners
the way you spoil me rotten
you teeth shining like coins in the city lights—
heaven is a night on earth with you

we can ride on cloud nine back to your apartment
where you'll undo your belt
wrap it around my throat
and tell me no one will love me better
than you do.

[my pulse]

so he's got a mood now
and he's treating me like shit
shouldn't he? I'm not his woman
wouldn't say his friend either
but he needs me like his two a.m. tipple

and I don't want to change him
I don't want him to turn into something he's not
as far as I'm concerned I
could as well make him worse and he says I'm damn good
at it

so he's in a mood now and
he says it's my fault
his pulse is beating out of time
he'll never be clean enough.

[sad girl pop]

he hasn't changed since the last time he apologized
and I'm afraid neither have I
but our letters are masterpieces
and our sex is art
he's a dagger in my head
that fills the crack of my broken mind.

[overdrive]

half a tank of fuel
hands wet on the wheel
racing in the lights for
who's not waiting for me

I watch my mind burn down
the rearview sees me
speeding down fire pit
laughing at the sparks.

[antisocial]

cheesy
motivational quote
shamelessly
passed off
as

- poetry

[#idiosyncrasy]

meal prep, self-care
hydratation, resilience
good vibes only, go outside
Live-Laugh-Love, promo code

detox tea, lifestyle coach
productivity, wisdom pearls
energy, the Universe,
so politically correct

motivation, awareness week
fitness guru, night routine
self-help books, free yoga class.
be yourself—wait, not like that!

[pigs]

there's a party tonight at the pigsty
like it's the end of 1999
the pigs are overexcited
happy as a pig in mud

the abundance is embarrassing:
tons of mushy peas, canned ravioli
scotch eggs and pigs in blankets 'cause
cannibalism was once socially acceptable
now it's turned into socially expected

them pigs mix warm beer from Poundland
with wine in carton boxes
homemade gin from down the cellar
with counterfeit Dior perfume

there's an orgy on the dance floor
to music louder than ten thousand drills
laughter's louder than bombs over Belgrade
sponsored by rotten.com

them pigs, they scream and oink, they ejaculate and howl
amazed by the greatness
of their own astonishing filth.

[iconoclast]

picture yourself holy.
your sacred heart on fire.
frankincense dripping from your empty eyes, beaded in
pearl reproduction of tears.
picture yourself.
eight men carrying you on their shoulders, on a cushion of
velvet and satin. in an ivory palanquin.
glimmering jewels on your marmoreal arms.
silver and diamonds on your big white hands.
picture yourself crowned in a halo of gold.
light shining on your alabaster cheeks. porcelain lips.
somebody could swear she did smile.
picture yourself before the crowd.
above tons of genuflecting flesh bowed down in prayer.
above endless streams of devotion.
above worshipers and their unconditional love.
picture yourself holy. divine. celestial. pure.
and now bleed for me.

[hello]

The super rich get super richer and the poor follow them on Twitter.
The most sensible statements lately
are coming from the Pope and Britney Spears.
The prime minister said he firmly believes in guardian angels
and the crowd cheered and clapped
as if the plane had finally landed.

Workers pledge allegiance to the brand they work for less than minimum wage.
Somebody's name is printed on my underwear.
The streets are full of people who are dead but nobody told them yet.
The Brits are mad at Brexit.
the French at everything.
Italians are mad at food.
Russians can't say anything.
There are eight billion of us, and we're all obsessed with the idea
of being understood.

I've just asked what's up

I told you what's up.

[somedays]

somedays I wake up with stones in my chest
with lakes in my lungs that won't make it to my eyes
detached from reality
aloof and quite dazed
I pray for bathwater to flush me down the drain.

somedays the fog in my head won't take any shape
slow-motion, no contact between brain and hands
my tongue's wings are pinned on the wall
trembling and fighting agains the iron nails

god, you depress me—she says, scrolling through her phone.

[purge]

I sit on front of the blank page
till something comes up
eventually
till something comes out
of my lungs
of my stomach
of my open wounds
I spray body fluids on paper
in the shape of language.

[birds]

I dream to be on a roof somewhere
higher than life
with peacocks' feathers caressing my skin
flamingos kissing my eyelids
owls reading Bukowski
and vultures eating away
all my rotten parts.

[black coffee]

I put a spell on you
as a heavy rain drums on the window
an old record spins
my cup of hot black coffee burns my fingertips
and my eyes bleed water for
all of that cigarette smoke

love will tear us apart (again)
and nobody ever taught me how to deal with myself
(on the other hand no one said they had to)

I put a spell on you, now
but one day, I know
I will be gloriously beautiful
like a god.

[washing machines]

the Chinese lady takes my change and taps on the till
managing a launderette washed her smile away
but the lucky cat in the neon lights
democratically waves at everyone:
the skinny old woman with her two Aldi bags
the young fat one
her three children she cannot control

the worn-out rider just happy to be sitting down
the guy pretending he's not drunk
the one here for the first time
because his technician forgot about their appointment
he hopes that's the last time too

humans spinning and cycling
at thirty degrees or more
unremovable stains
all equal before the wall
of industrial portholes.

[closed for inventory]

I've locked myself out of the apartment. No better time for
me to shut down as well and take account of all that's
wrong with me:

my nose is quite big
I didn't get that role last year
I've never watched *Game of Thrones*
I didn't get *Donnie Darko*

I don't have any clean socks
I've never finished *Anna Karenina*
today's a bad hair day
Jane Birkin's not my grandma

a drunken hobo yelled at me (but it was probably my
fault)
my best relationship lasted less than twelve months
I embarrassed myself that day in tenth grade
my phone is ringing but it's certainly spam

guess I'll just sit here and wait for someone to come
I'll be wasting my time without home or keys
watching passersby busy with their own inventories
but to quote a wiser woman "you might as well live."

[this is not a poem]

if there's one thing
I really don't like about my body
is that I was born with just
one middle finger per hand.

[butterflies underground]

in bloom at night
club kids Manchester
Liverpool
Birmingham
tripping on lights
moths to lightbulbs
drumbeats
diet coke + vodka
rattling studs
sugary sweat
mass production of shooting stars
our silver will never rust.

[life choices on sunday morning]

from tomorrow I'll be peaceful and content
and I won't choke on my own expectations
my hair will be mid-length and well-groomed
and my clothes will smell like brand conditioner.

from tomorrow I'll moisturize compulsively
and my eyeliner will always be on point
I won't put spicy oil on everything I eat
and my breath will be so fresh you'll wish to die in my throat.

from tomorrow my dishes will never form a curious pile in the sink
I'll buy new clothes and find a real job
I'll download Tinder and swipe right to decency
and carry his healthy child in my womb.

from tomorrow I'll be okay
you won't even recognize me.
today, however,
I've got my finger on the trigger
and you're in my way.

[to-do list]

accept candy from a stranger
take a deep breath
burn away like a shooting star
blink your eyes and she's gone

come back as one of Nabokov's butterflies
useless and beautiful
beautifully useless and
perfectly content

wishing for nothing more.

[last prayer]

Virgin Mary
rub your fingers
softly through my hair
read me Majakovskij to sleep.

[light blue]

get me the golden hour in a flute of champagne
liquid sunset to sip on a rooftop
above all the traffic and trivialities
just below the blue vault.

[astrophilia]

night sky pierced throughoutly
of silver and gold
and I am
spread on the rooftop
eyes to the infinity
legs open
screaming for more.

Ackowledgements

Thanks to Anton Bonnici and Genna Rivieccio of *The Opiate*, without whom this book wouldn't have been possible. Thanks to David Barnes and the whole Spoken Word Paris community, in which I found my tribe. Thanks to Jess and Maher a.k.a. my guardian angels. Thanks to Stefan Dolhain for keeping me under his wing during my first months in the French capital, and for encouraging my art while teaching me a lot. Thanks to *Paris Lit Up*, *Tint Journal*, *The Argyle*, *Sad Girl Review*, *Our Verse* and *OpenDoor*, who published my work before this book happened.

About the Author

Chiara Maxia is an actress and writer originally from Sardinia. She has lived in different places, including England, Moscow and Paris, where she graduated in Film Acting. She now lives between France and Italy. Her work has appeared in numerous literary journals, including *The Opiate, Tint Journal, The Argyle, Paris Lit Up, OpenDoor* and *Our Verse*.

www.ingramcontent.com/pod-product-compliance
Lightning Source LLC
LaVergne TN
LVHW030951110526
838202LV00091BA/6437